O'Keeffe

by Iain Gray

D1324581

Lang**Syne**

PUBLISHING

WRITING *to* REMEMBER

LangSyne

PUBLISHING

WRITING *to* REMEMBER

Office 5, Vineyard Business Centre,
Pathhead, Midlothian EH37 5XP
Tel: 01875 321 203 Fax: 01875 321 233
E-mail: info@lang-syne.co.uk
www.langsyneshop.co.uk

Design by Dorothy Meikle
Printed by Hay Nisbet Press, Glasgow
© Lang Syne Publishers Ltd 2009

ISBN 978-1-85217-323-4

O'Keeffe

MOTTO:
Nothing is difficult
to the brave and faithful.

CREST:
A griffin grasping
a sword in its right paw.

NAME variations include:
Ó Caoimh (*Gaelic*)
O'Keefe
Coemh
Coohm
Keefe
Keeffe

Chapter one:
Origins of Irish surnames

**According to an old saying, there are two types of Irish –
those who actually are Irish and those who wish they were.**

This sentiment is only one example of the allure that the
high romance and drama of the proud nation's history holds
for thousands of people scattered across the world today.

It's a sad fact, however, that the vast majority of Irish
surnames are found far beyond Irish shores, rather than on
the Emerald Isle itself.

The population stood at around eight million souls in
1841, but today it stands at fewer than six million.

This is mainly a tragic consequence of the potato
famine, also known as the Great Hunger, which devastated
Ireland between 1845 and 1849.

The Irish peasantry had become almost wholly reliant
for basic sustenance on the potato, first introduced from the
Americas in the seventeenth century.

When the crop was hit by a blight, at least 800,000
people starved to death while an estimated two million
others were forced to seek a new life far from their native
shores – particularly in America, Canada, and Australia.

The effects of the potato blight continued until about
1851, by which time a firm pattern of emigration had
become established.

Ireland's loss, however, was to the gain of the countries in which the immigrants settled, contributing enormously, as their descendants do today, to the well being of the nations in which their forefathers settled.

But those who were forced through dire circumstance to establish a new life in foreign parts never forgot their roots, or the proud heritage and traditions of the land that gave them birth.

Nor do their descendants.

It is a heritage that is inextricably bound up in the colourful variety of Irish names themselves – and the origin and history of these names forms an integral part of the vibrant drama that is the nation's history, one of both glorious fortune and tragic misfortune.

This history is well documented, and one of the most important and fascinating of the earliest sources are *The Annals of the Four Masters*, compiled between 1632 and 1636 by four friars at the Franciscan Monastery in County Donegal.

Compiled from earlier sources, and purporting to go back to the Biblical Deluge, much of the material takes in the mythological origins and history of Ireland and the Irish.

This includes tales of successive waves of invaders and settlers such as the Fomorians, the Partholonians, the Nemedians, the Fir Bolgs, the Tuatha De Danann, and the Laigain.

Of particular interest are the *Milesian Genealogies*,

because the majority of Irish clans today claim a descent from either Heremon, Ir, or Heber – three of the sons of Milesius, a king of what is now modern day Spain.

These sons invaded Ireland in the second millennium B.C, apparently in fulfilment of a mysterious prophecy received by their father.

This Milesian lineage is said to have ruled Ireland for nearly 3,000 years, until the island came under the sway of England's King Henry II in 1171 following what is known as the Cambro-Norman invasion.

This is an important date not only in Irish history in general, but for the effect the invasion subsequently had for Irish surnames.

'Cambro' comes from the Welsh, and 'Cambro-Norman' describes those Welsh knights of Norman origin who invaded Ireland.

But they were invaders who stayed, inter-marrying with the native Irish population and founding their own proud dynasties that bore Cambro-Norman names such as Archer, Barbour, Brannagh, Fitzgerald, Fitzgibbon, Fleming, Joyce, Plunkett, and Walsh – to name only a few.

These 'Cambro-Norman' surnames that still flourish throughout the world today form one of the three main categories in which Irish names can be placed – those of Gaelic-Irish, Cambro-Norman, and Anglo-Irish.

Previous to the Cambro-Norman invasion of the twelfth century, and throughout the earlier invasions and settlement of those wild bands of sea rovers known as the Vikings in the eighth and ninth centuries, the population of the island was relatively small, and it was normal for a person to be identified through the use of only a forename.

But as population gradually increased and there were many more people with the same forename, surnames were adopted to distinguish one person, or one community, from another.

Individuals identified themselves with their own particular tribe, or 'tuath', and this tribe – that also became known as a clann, or clan – took its name from some distinguished ancestor who had founded the clan.

The Gaelic-Irish form of the name Kelly, for example, is Ó Ceallaigh, or O'Kelly, indicating descent from an original 'Ceallaigh', with the 'O' denoting 'grandson of.' The name was later anglicised to Kelly.

The prefix 'Mac' or 'Mc', meanwhile, as with the clans of the Scottish Highlands, denotes 'son of.'

Although the Irish clans had much in common with their Scottish counterparts, one important difference lies in what are known as 'septs', or branches, of the clan.

Septs of Scottish clans were groups who often bore an entirely different name from the clan name but were under the clan's protection.

In Ireland, septs were groups that shared the same name and who could be found scattered throughout the four provinces of Ulster, Leinster, Munster, and Connacht.

The 'golden age' of the Gaelic-Irish clans, infused as their veins were with the blood of Celts, pre-dates the Viking invasions of the eighth and ninth centuries and the Norman invasion of the twelfth century, and the sacred heart of the country was the Hill of Tara, near the River Boyne, in County Meath.

Known in Gaelic as 'Teamhar na Rí', or Hill of Kings, it was the royal seat of the 'Ard Rí Éireann', or High King of Ireland, to whom the petty kings, or chieftains, from the island's provinces were ultimately subordinate.

It was on the Hill of Tara, beside a stone pillar known as the Irish 'Lia Fáil', or Stone of Destiny, that the High Kings were inaugurated and, according to legend, this stone would emit a piercing screech that could be heard all over Ireland when touched by the hand of the rightful king.

The Hill of Tara is today one of the island's main tourist attractions.

Opposition to English rule over Ireland, established in the wake of the Cambro-Norman invasion, broke out frequently and the harsh solution adopted by the powerful forces of the Crown was to forcibly evict the native Irish from their lands.

These lands were then granted to Protestant colonists, or 'planters', from Britain.

Many of these colonists, ironically, came from Scotland and were the descendants of the original 'Scotti', or 'Scots', who gave their name to Scotland after migrating there in the fifth century A.D., from the north of Ireland.

Colonisation entailed harsh penal laws being imposed on the majority of the native Irish population, stripping them practically of all of their rights.

The Crown's main bastion in Ireland was Dublin and its environs, known as the Pale, and it was the dispossessed peasantry who lived outside this Pale, desperately striving to eke out a meagre living.

It was this that gave rise to the modern-day expression of someone or something being 'beyond the pale'.

Attempts were made to stamp out all aspects of the ancient Gaelic-Irish culture, to the extent that even to bear a Gaelic-Irish name was to invite discrimination.

This is why many Gaelic-Irish names were anglicised with, for example, and noted above, Ó Ceallaigh, or O'Kelly, being anglicised to Kelly.

Succeeding centuries have seen strong revivals of Gaelic-Irish consciousness, however, and this has led to many families reverting back to the original form of their name, while the language itself is frequently found on the fluent tongues of an estimated 90,000 to 145,000 of the island's population.

Ireland's turbulent history of religious and political strife is one that lasted well into the twentieth century, a landmark century that saw the partition of the island into the twenty-six counties of the independent Republic of

Ireland, or Eire, and the six counties of Northern Ireland, or Ulster.

Dublin, originally founded by Vikings, is now a vibrant and truly cosmopolitan city while the proud city of Belfast is one of the jewels in the crown of Ulster.

It was Saint Patrick who first brought the light of Christianity to Ireland in the fifth century A.D.

Interpretations of this Christian message have varied over the centuries, often leading to bitter sectarian conflict – but the many intricately sculpted Celtic Crosses found all over the island are symbolic of a unity that crosses the sectarian divide.

It is an image that fuses the 'old gods' of the Celts with Christianity.

All the signs from the early years of this new millennium indicate that sectarian strife may soon become a thing of the past – with the Irish and their many kinsfolk across the world, be they Protestant or Catholic, finding common purpose in the rich tapestry of their shared heritage.

Chapter two:

The hospitable land

Present day County Cork in Munster, which along with Ulster, Leinster and Connacht makes up the four ancient provinces of Ireland, was from earliest times the homeland of bearers of the O'Keeffe name.

A name with several spelling variations, the most common form found on the Emerald Isle today is 'O'Keeffe', with two 'fs', while the 'O'Keefe' form, with only one 'f' is found mainly in North America – although this is certainly not a hard and fast rule.

The Gaelic-Irish rendering of the name is Ó Caoimh, derived from 'caomh', indicating 'kind', 'gentle' or 'noble' – and the original 'Caomh' was the late ninth century Art Caomh, son of a Munster king known as Fionghuine.

Fionghuine was also known as the Lord, or Prince, of Fermoy – with what is now the barony of Fermoy in Co. Cork their main centre.

Further ennobling the O'Keeffe bloodline is that they are of direct descent from the third century warrior king Olioll Olum who, in turn, was in a line of descent from Ireland's very earliest monarchs.

This was through Heber who, along with Heremon, Ir, Amergin and four other brothers, was a son of Milesius – a king of what is now modern day Spain, and who had planned to invade Ireland in fulfilment of a mysterious prophecy.

Milesius died before he could embark on the invasion but his sons, including Heber, Ir, Heremon and Amergin, successfully undertook the daunting task in his stead.

Legend holds that their invasion fleet was scattered in a storm and Ir killed when his ship was driven onto the island of Scellig-Mhicheal, off the coast of modern day Co. Kerry.

Only Heremon, Heber, and Amergin survived, although Ir left issue.

Heremon and Heber became the first of the Milesian monarchs of Ireland, but Heremon later killed Heber in a quarrel said to have been caused by their wives, while Amergin was slain by Heremon in an argument over territory.

Along with the O'Keeffes, other clans that trace a descent from Heber include those of Brady, Brennan, Carroll, Doran, O'Brien, O'Connor, O'Hara, O'Neill and O'Sullivan.

Glen Amhain, now known as Glanworth, and what was known as Urluachra were the main bases of the O'Keeffes of Fermoy.

It was rich territory, and the Irish annals record how:

O'Keeffe of the brown and handsome brows,
Is Chief of Urluachra of the fertile lands,
The inheritor of the land hospitable,
Which vies in beauty with the fair plains of Meath.

But although it could not have been foreseen at the time, the fortunes of native Irish clans such as the O'Keeffes were destined to spiral into decline and their ancient way of life was all but extinguished.

Ireland by the twelfth century was far from being a unified nation, split up as it was into territories ruled over by squabbling chieftains who ruled as kings in their own right – and this inter-clan rivalry ultimately proved disastrous as it worked to the advantage of invaders.

In a series of bloody conflicts one chieftain, or king, would occasionally gain the upper hand over his rivals, and by 1156 the most powerful was Muirchertach MacLochlainn, king of the O'Neills.

He was opposed by the equally powerful Rory O'Connor, king of the province of Connacht, but he increased his power and influence by allying himself with Dermot MacMurrough, King of Leinster.

MacLochlainn and MacMurrough were aware that the main key to the kingdom of Ireland was the thriving trading port of Dublin that had been established by invading Vikings, or Ostmen in 852 A.D.

Their combined forces took the port, but when MacLochlainn died the Dubliners rose up in revolt and overthrew the unpopular MacMurrough.

A triumphant Rory O'Connor entered Dublin and was later inaugurated as Ard Rí, but MacMurrough refused to accept defeat.

He appealed for help from England's Henry II in unseating O'Connor, an act that was to radically affect the future course of Ireland's fortunes.

The English monarch agreed to help MacMurrough, but distanced himself from direct action by delegating his Norman subjects in Wales with the task.

These ambitious and battle-hardened barons and knights had first settled in Wales following the Norman Conquest of England in 1066 and, with an eye on rich booty, plunder and lands, were only too eager to obey their sovereign's wishes and furnish MacMurrough with aid.

MacMurrough crossed the Irish Sea to Bristol, where he rallied powerful barons such as Robert Fitzstephen and Maurice Fitzgerald to his cause, along with Gilbert de Clare, Earl of Pembroke, also known as Strongbow.

As an inducement to Strongbow, MacMurrough offered him the hand of his beautiful young daughter, Aife, in marriage, with the further sweetener to the deal that he would take over the province of Leinster on MacMurrough's death.

The mighty Norman war machine soon moved into action, and so fierce and disciplined was their onslaught on the forces of Rory O'Connor and his allies that by 1171 they had recaptured Dublin, in the name of MacMurrough, and other strategically important territories.

Henry II now began to take cold feet over the venture, realising that he may have created a rival in the form of a separate Norman kingdom in Ireland.

Accordingly, he landed on the island, near Waterford, at the head of a large army with the aim of curbing the power of his Cambro-Norman barons.

But protracted war was averted when the barons submitted to the royal will, promising homage and allegiance in return for holding the territories they had conquered in the king's name.

Henry also received the submission and homage of many of the Irish chieftains, tired as they were with internecine warfare and also perhaps realising that as long as they were rivals and not united they were no match for the powerful forces the English Crown could muster.

English dominion over Ireland was ratified through the Treaty of Windsor of 1175, under the terms of which Rory O'Connor, for example, was allowed to rule territory unoccupied by the Normans in the role of a vassal of the king.

Two years earlier, Pope Alexander III had given Papal sanction to Henry's dominance over Ireland, on condition that he uphold the rights of the Holy Roman Catholic Church and that chieftains such as O'Connor adhere rigorously to the oaths of fealty they had sworn to the English king.

But the land was far from unified, blighted as it was with years of warfare and smarting under many grievances.

There were actually three separate Irelands.

These were the territories of the privileged and powerful

Norman barons and their retainers, the Ireland of the disaffected Gaelic-Irish who held lands unoccupied by the Normans, and the Pale – comprised of Dublin itself and a substantial area of its environs ruled over by an English elite.

An Anglo-Norman invasion of the island followed in the wake of the Cambro-Norman invasion, as ambitious Norman families and adventurers flooded in.

This was to the cost of many native Irish clans who found themselves inexorably pushed from their lands.

Among the victims were the O'Keeffes, who were expelled westwards out of Fermoy by the mighty Norman family of Roche.

The O'Keeffes found themselves in the barony of Dunhallow, where their seat was at Dromagh in the parish of Dromtarriff.

This area became known as Pobal O'Keeffe, and it is an indication of the indelible mark that the O'Keeffes impressed upon it that it is still known by the same name to this day.

Gallingly for the O'Keeffes, however, their previous territory of Fermoy eventually became known as Roche's Country, with the Roches in control as Viscounts of Fermoy.

Chapter three:

Rebellion and atrocity

Devastation visited Ireland again in 1641 when landowners rebelled against the English Crown's policy of settling, or 'planting' loyal Protestants on Irish land.

This policy had started during the reign from 1491 to 1547 of Henry VIII, whose Reformation effectively outlawed the established Roman Catholic faith throughout his dominions.

In the insurrection that exploded in 1641, at least 2,000 Protestant settlers were massacred while thousands more were stripped of their belongings and driven from their lands to seek refuge where they could.

England had its own distractions with the Civil War that culminated in the execution of Charles I in 1649, and from 1641 to 1649 Ireland was ruled by a rebel group known as the Irish Catholic Confederation, or the Confederation of Kilkenny.

One prominent rebel was the O'Keeffe chief Domhnall O'Keeffe of Dromagh, and he and his family were destined to suffer dearly for their stance.

Terrible as the atrocities against the Protestant settlers had been, subsequent accounts became greatly exaggerated, serving to fuel a burning desire for revenge against the rebels.

The English Civil War intervened to prevent immediate action, but following the execution of Charles I and the consolidation of the power of England's Oliver Cromwell, the time was ripe for revenge.

Cromwell descended on Ireland at the head of a 20,000-strong army that landed at Ringford, near Dublin, in August of 1649.

He had three main aims:

To quash all forms of rebellion, to 'remove' all Catholic landowners who had taken part in the rebellion, and to convert the native Irish to the Protestant faith.

An early warning of the terrors that were in store came when the northeastern town of Drogheda was stormed and taken in September and between 2,000 and 4,000 of its inhabitants killed.

The defenders of Drogheda's St. Peter's Church, who had refused to surrender, were burned to death as they huddled for refuge in the steeple and the church was deliberately torched.

A similar fate descended on Wexford, on the southeast coast, where at least 1,500 of its inhabitants were slaughtered, including 200 defenceless women, despite their pathetic pleas for mercy.

Cromwell soon held the land in a grip of iron, allowing him to implement what amounted to a policy of ethnic cleansing.

His troopers were given free rein to hunt down and kill

priests, while rebel estates were confiscated, including those of the O'Keeffes.

An estimated 11 million acres of land were confiscated and the dispossessed banished to Connacht and Co. Clare, while an edict was issued stating that any native Irish found east of the River Shannon after May 1, 1654, faced either summary execution or transportation to the West Indies.

Domhnall O'Keeffe survived until 1655, while his son, Captain Daniel O'Keeffe, took up the banner of revolt more than thirty years later.

This was in what is known as Cogadh an Dá Rí, or The War of the Two Kings.

Also known as the Williamite War in Ireland, it was sparked off when the Stuart monarch James II, under threat from powerful factions who feared a return to the dominance of Roman Catholicism under his rule, fled into French exile in 1688.

The Protestant William of Orange and his wife Mary were invited to take up the throne – but James had significant Catholic support in Ireland.

His supporters were known as Jacobites, and among them was Captain Daniel O'Keeffe.

Following the arrival in England of William and Mary from Holland, Richard Talbot, 1st Earl of Tyrconnell and James's Lord Deputy in Ireland, assembled an army loyal to the Stuart cause.

The aim was to garrison and fortify the island in the

name of James and quell any resistance – but Londonderry, or Derry, proved loyal to the cause of William of Orange, or William III as he had become, and managed to hold out against a siege that was not lifted until July 28, 1689.

James, with the support of troops and money supplied by Louis XIV of France, had landed at Kinsale in March of 1689 and joined forces with his Irish supporters.

A series of military encounters followed, culminating in James's defeat by an army commanded by William at the battle of the Boyne on July 12, 1690.

James fled again into French exile, never to return, while the remnants of his demoralised army retreated to Limerick, in the west.

A Williamite siege of Limerick was repulsed by its defenders in August of 1690, and William's army retreated from the west in favour of consolidating a hold over the less strongly defended southern reaches of the island.

They managed to take the strategically important southern ports of Kinsale and Cork under an army commanded by the Earl of Marlborough, while William himself left the island later in the year after turning over command of his forces to the Dutch General Godert de Ginkell.

These forces took most of the province of Connacht after successfully besieging the town of Athlone and, having consolidated their position there, began to advance on the Jacobite strongholds of Limerick and Galway.

A Jacobite force under the French commander St. Ruth attempted to block their advance at Aughrim on July 12, 1691, only to be defeated in a battle that left about half of the Jacobite army of 16,000 men either killed, wounded or taken prisoner.

Among the many Jacobite dead on the field of battle was St. Ruth himself and Captain Daniel O'Keeffe, last chief of that line of the family.

Galway later surrendered to de Ginkell, while Limerick was forced into surrender on September 23.

A peace treaty known as the Treaty of Limerick followed, under which those Jacobites willing to swear an oath of loyalty to William were allowed to remain in their native land.

Those reluctant to do so, including many native Irish such as the O'Keeffes, chose foreign exile.

The O'Keeffe lands were confiscated and sold only a few years after the signing of the Treaty of Limerick.

One of the many noted chroniclers of these troubled times was Father Eoghan O'Keeffe, who was born in 1656 and died in 1726.

President of the bards, or poets, of North Cork, his compositions are still recited and sung by Cork natives to this day.

A further flight overseas occurred following an abortive rebellion in 1798, while O'Keeffes were also among the many thousands of Irish who were forced to emigrate during the famine known as The Great Hunger, caused by a failure of the potato crop between 1845 and 1849.

But Ireland's loss of sons and daughters such as the O'Keeffes was in many cases to the gain of those nations in which they settled.

Chapter four:

On the world stage

Bearers of the O'Keeffe name, in all its variety of spellings, have gained distinction in a colourful variety of pursuits.

Born in 1928 on an isolated farm near Warrnambool, about three hours drive from Melbourne, **Peggy O'Keefe** is the pianist who established a successful career for herself after arriving in Britain from her native Australia in 1960 and later taking British citizenship.

A graduate of Melbourne University Music Conservatory, where she studied harp, violin, piano and singing, she was drawn to the thriving jazz nightclub and cabaret scene of early 1960s London.

It was here that she played piano for, and became friends with, international stars who included Tony Bennett, Cleo Laine, Sammy Davis Jr. and Dizzy Gillespie.

In 1962 she was offered a six-month contract with the Scottish-based Reo Stakis hotel empire to become resident pianist in its Chevalier Casino in Glasgow.

The six-month contract extended to six years, during which time she played with her own jazz trio while also working for both BBC and Scottish Television.

By 1968 she was working almost full-time as a pianist for both stations – an activity that carried on until the 1980s.

In the latter stages of her career she continued to play with her own trio while also playing piano for special music programmes of orchestras that included the Royal Scottish National Orchestra.

A fellow Australian musician, but one of a decidedly wilder nature, was **Johnny O'Keefe**, the rock and roll singer who was born in 1935 in Sydney.

Nicknamed 'The Wild One' in recognition of both his hit single of the same name from 1958 and for his off-stage antics, he released more than 50 singles and 100 albums over a 20-year career that ended with his death in 1978.

Still recognised as Australia's most successful chart performer, he was also the first Australian rock and roll performer to tour the United States.

A special Australian stamp was issued in 1998 in recognition of his contribution to the early years of rock and roll.

In a different musical genre **Padraig O'Keeffe**, born in 1887 in Castleisland, Co. Kerry, was the noted Irish traditional musician who was taught to play the fiddle as a child by an uncle.

Following in his father's footsteps, he trained as a schoolteacher, but left the profession in 1920 for a career as a fiddle player and instructor. He died in 1963 – and every year since 1993 the Padraig O'Keeffe Traditional Music Festival has been held in his native Castleisland.

Also in Ireland **Eoin O'Keeffe**, born in 1979 in Clonmel, is the Irish composer whose compositions have been performed at prestigious festivals such as the 2006 City of London Festival and the 2007 New Music Festival at London's Guidhall.

From the world of music to the world of acting, **Jodi O'Keefe** is the American actress who was born in 1978 in Cliffwood Beach, New Jersey.

Her first major role was at the age of 17 as actor Don Johnson's daughter Cassidy Bridges on the *Nash Bridges* television series.

She has also appeared in series that include *Charmed*.

Born in 1954 in Ripley, Tennessee, **Miles O'Keeffe** is the American film and television actor whose first major role was as Tarzan in the 1981 film version of *Tarzan, the Ape Man*, while other films in which he has appeared include the 1982 *Ator, The Fighting Eagle*, the 1995 *Zero Tolerance* and, from 2005, *The Unknown*.

A nephew of the late Australian rock and roll musician Johnny O'Keefe and a son of the former New South Wales Supreme Court Judge Barry O'Keefe, **Andrew O'Keefe** is the Australian television personality and games show host who was born in 1971 in Sydney.

Nominated in 2004 for Australia's Logie Award for Best New Male Talent and in 2005 for Most Popular Presenter, he is best known as the host of the Australian version of the game show *Deal or No Deal*.

O'Keeffes have also gained prominence in the creative world of art.

Born in 1797 in Fermoy, Co. Cork, **John O'Keeffe** was the noted Irish portrait painter whose rather unlikely introduction to the world of art was as an apprentice coach painter.

More creatively, he began painting scenes for local theatres before turning his talents to painting religious pictures for Roman Catholic churches.

Leaving his native Cork for Dublin in 1834, he successfully exhibited a series of portrait and subject paintings, while his 1835 *A Sibyl* is now one of the prized exhibits in the Museum of Cork.

Born in 1887 in Sun Prairie, Wisconsin, **Georgia O'Keeffe** is recognised as having been one of the most influential figures in American art.

Best known for her landscape paintings of the American Southwest and of New Mexico, where she settled and lived until her death in 1986, she was elected to the American Academy of Arts and Letters in 1962, while the Georgia O'Keeffe Museum was established in Santa Fe in 1997.

An important figure in New Zealand art history, **Alfred O'Keeffe** was the artist and teacher born in 1858 in Victoria, Australia.

Moving to New Zealand with his family at the age of seven, he later studied at the Dunedin School of Art and in Paris.

Two of his sons were killed during the First World War and this tragedy led to him painting his famous *The Defence*

Minister's Telegram, depicting a father receiving news of his son's death and which is now in Dunedin's Public Art Gallery.

In the world of politics, Bartholomew O'Keeffe is the Irish Fiana Fáil politician better known as **Batt O'Keeffe**.

Born in 1945 in Cullen, Co. Cork, at the time of writing he is the Republic of Ireland's Minister for Education and Science.

In the competitive world of sport, **Kerry O'Keeffe** is the former top Australian cricketer also known as Skulls O'Keeffe.

Born in 1949 in Hurtsville, New South Wales, the former spin bowler played 24 Tests between 1971 and 1977 and is now a popular cricket commentator for radio.

In the world of literature, **John O'Keeffe** was the dramatist who had the distinction of being the most produced playwright in London in the final decades of the eighteenth century.

Born in 1747, he wrote a number of highly successful farces, including the 1778 *Lumpkin in Town* and the 1791 *Wild Oats* – most recently revived for the stage in the 1990s.

Recognised as having been one of the most important publishing editors of the twentieth century, **Timothy O'Keeffe** was the Irish editor and publisher born in Kinsale, Co. Cork, in 1926 and who died in 1994.

Forming the publishing house of Martin, Brian and O'Keeffe, he was later responsible for the re-publication of

Flann O'Brien's noted *At Swim-Two-Birds* in addition to the posthumous publication in 1967 of O'Brien's *The Third Policeman*.

One particularly adventurous bearer of the name was **David O'Keefe**, born in about 1824 in Ireland and who later immigrated to America and settled in Savannah, Georgia.

Filled with wanderlust, the seafaring O'Keefe left the United States in 1871 for the South Pacific – only to be shipwrecked off Yap, one of the Caroline Islands.

Rescued by the islanders, he quickly spotted the commercial potential of what are known as Rai stones – large circular stone disks carved out of limestone by the islanders which were used as a form of currency.

Sending to Savannah for iron tools, he helped the islanders to quarry the stones, in return receiving valuable products such as copra that he exported to great profit to himself throughout the Far East.

Thanks to his immense wealth and influence he came to 'own' the island of Yap, and married a native woman although he had a wife and children back in Savannah.

He died in 1901 on a sea voyage back to Savannah, and is memorably portrayed by Burt Lancaster in the 1954 movie *His Majesty O'Keefe*.

Another enterprising bearer of the name was the entrepreneur and philanthropist **Eugene O'Keefe**, born in 1827 in Bandon, Co. Cork, and who died in 1913.

Moving to Canada with his parents when he was aged

five, his first job was with the Toronto Savings Bank, while he later became president of the Home Bank of Canada.

In 1891 he founded the famed O'Keefe Brewery Company of Toronto Ltd; later selling the business following the death of his son in 1911.

Two years earlier he had become the first Canadian layman to be made a private Papal chamberlain – in recognition of his charitable work on behalf of the Roman Catholic Church.

In addition to building no less than five churches in Toronto and the St. Augustine's Seminary in Scarsborough, he also built the city's first low-income housing development.

Reaching for the stars **John O'Keefe** was the American planetary scientist credited with the discovery of the earth's 'pear' shape, following his analysis of special data collected from satellites in the late 1950s.

Born in 1916, he worked from 1958 to 1995 with the American space agency NASA and was a driving force behind the agency's science programme.

He died in 2000.

Born in 1956, **Sean O'Keefe** is the former Secretary of the U.S. Navy from 1992 to 1993 who also served as administrator of NASA from 2001 to 2005.

It is in recognition of his vision and leadership in advancing the spirit of space exploration during his tenure as administrator, that Asteroid 78905 Seanokeefe is named in his honour.

Key dates in Ireland's history from the first settlers to the formation of the Irish Republic:

circa 7000 B.C.	Arrival and settlement of Stone Age people.
circa 3000 B.C.	Arrival of settlers of New Stone Age period.
circa 600 B.C.	First arrival of the Celts.
200 A.D.	Establishment of Hill of Tara, Co. Meath, as seat of the High Kings.
circa 432 A.D.	Christian mission of St. Patrick.
800-920 A.D.	Invasion and subsequent settlement of Vikings.
1002 A.D.	Brian Boru recognised as High King.
1014	Brian Boru killed at battle of Clontarf.
1169-1170	Cambro-Norman invasion of the island.
1171	Henry II claims Ireland for the English Crown.
1366	Statutes of Kilkenny ban marriage between native Irish and English.
1529-1536	England's Henry VIII embarks on religious Reformation.
1536	Earl of Kildare rebels against the Crown.
1541	Henry VIII declared King of Ireland.
1558	Accession to English throne of Elizabeth I.
1565	Battle of Affane.
1569-1573	First Desmond Rebellion.
1579-1583	Second Desmond Rebellion.
1594-1603	Nine Years War.
1606	Plantation' of Scottish and English settlers.
1607	Flight of the Earls.
1632-1636	Annals of the Four Masters compiled.
1641	Rebellion over policy of plantation and other grievances.
1649	Beginning of Cromwellian conquest.
1688	Flight into exile in France of Catholic Stuart monarch James II as Protestant Prince William of Orange invited to take throne of England along with his wife, Mary.
1689	William and Mary enthroned as joint monarchs; siege of Derry.
1690	Jacobite forces of James defeated by William at battle of the Boyne (July) and Dublin taken.

1691	Athlone taken by William; Jacobite defeats follow at Aughrim, Galway, and Limerick; conflict ends with Treaty of Limerick (October) and Irish officers allowed to leave for France.
1695	Penal laws introduced to restrict rights of Catholics; banishment of Catholic clergy.
1704	Laws introduced constricting rights of Catholics in landholding and public office.
1728	Franchise removed from Catholics.
1791	Foundation of United Irishmen republican movement.
1796	French invasion force lands in Bantry Bay.
1798	Defeat of Rising in Wexford and death of United Irishmen leaders Wolfe Tone and Lord Edward Fitzgerald.
1800	Act of Union between England and Ireland.
1803	Dublin Rising under Robert Emmet.
1829	Catholics allowed to sit in Parliament.
1845-1849	The Great Hunger: thousands starve to death as potato crop fails and thousands more emigrate.
1856	Phoenix Society founded.
1858	Irish Republican Brotherhood established.
1873	Foundation of Home Rule League.
1893	Foundation of Gaelic League.
1904	Foundation of Irish Reform Association.
1913	Dublin strikes and lockout.
1916	Easter Rising in Dublin and proclamation of an Irish Republic.
1917	Irish Parliament formed after Sinn Fein election victory.
1919-1921	War between Irish Republican Army and British Army.
1922	Irish Free State founded, while six northern counties remain part of United Kingdom as Northern Ireland, or Ulster; civil war up until 1923 between rival republican groups.
1949	Foundation of Irish Republic after all remaining constitutional links with Britain are severed.